Find Your Happy

by Dr. Katie O'Connell
and Lisa Regan

ARCTURUS

For kids and parents finding their happy,
and for Lisa who found me.

ARCTURUS

This edition published in 2020 by Arcturus Publishing Limited
26/27 Bickels Yard, 151–153 Bermondsey Street,
London SE1 3HA

Authors: Dr. Katie O'Connell and Lisa Regan
Illustrator: Mel Howells
Editor: Donna Gregory
Designer: Jeni Child
Editorial Manager: Joe Harris
Design Manager: Jessica Holliland

ISBN: 978-1-78950-649-5
CH007198NT
Supplier 29, Date 0320, Print run 10175

Printed in China

Contents

Find Your Happy!

Life is full of ups and downs—it's totally normal not to be bursting with happiness all of the time. But if you feel like you're too sad, too often, this book can show you some ways that you can try to find your happy again.

It's important to feel and understand your emotions but it's not always wise to be led by them. Making yourself and others miserable is no way to be. Let's learn to explore your feelings and choose to react in a balanced way.

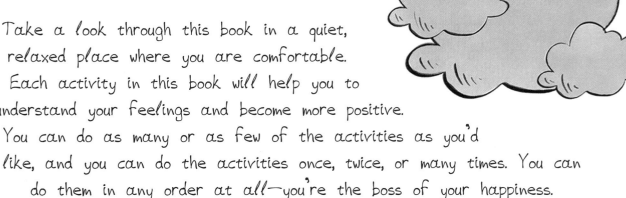

Take a look through this book in a quiet, relaxed place where you are comfortable. Each activity in this book will help you to understand your feelings and become more positive. You can do as many or as few of the activities as you'd like, and you can do the activities once, twice, or many times. You can do them in any order at all—you're the boss of your happiness.

Who can help you?

You don't have to struggle alone. Learning to manage your feelings is part of growing up. Nearly everyone you know, including your parents and teachers, has felt like you feel now (whatever that might be) at some point.

Don't be afraid to bring up your struggles with people you trust. This can be a relative, sibling, friend, teacher, or coach. Sometimes hearing about how other people manage their feelings gives us good ideas about what we can try and also helps us to not feel alone. It can be hard at first, but once you bring it up you will find many people who are working on finding their happy.

Set Yourself Some Feeling Goals

It's easy to say "I want to be happy," but what does that really mean?
What is important to you?

Apart from being happy, what would you like to feel? Here are some examples:

- I want to sleep well.

- I want to be able to deal with changes.

- I want to be good to myself.

- I want to be kind to others.

- I want to be strong.

- I want to be balanced.

- I want to be flexible.

- I want to burn off some energy.

Write down one or two feeling goals that really matter to you here:

Write down something that has affected your feelings recently:

_____

_____

If you're finding it hard to think of connections between things that have happened and how you've been feeling, here are some examples:

- You might feel sad if your friend played with somebody else instead of you.

- You might feel proud if you tried something new.

- You might feel upset if somebody you love has gone away.

- You might feel relieved if you did well on a test.

Can you think of something that you can do to help you achieve one of your feeling goals?

_____

_____

How it helps

Knowing the connections between your feelings, thoughts, and actions takes you away from being a robot and closer to being your super-smart, reflective self. Setting feeling goals is just as important as setting goals in any other area of your life. Set your own targets for how you want to feel and behave.

Listen to Your Body

Your body has chemicals inside that can turn you into a super-powered machine. The chemicals are there to help you survive; they make you run faster, think quicker, and get a buzz from doing the right thing. The chemicals show themselves on the inside and the outside of your body.

Are any of these familiar sensations?

☐ Dizzy	☐ Relaxed	☐ Annoyed
☐ Excited	☐ Shaky	☐ Loose
☐ Tingly	☐ Cold	☐ Bubbly
☐ Irritated	☐ Fuzzy	☐ Light
☐ Fluttery	☐ Calm	☐ Solid
☐ Jiggly	☐ Quiet	☐ Sick
☐ Sweaty	☐ Warm	☐ Soft
☐ Scared	☐ Numb	☐ Tense

The sensations in your body can become so strong that they move into your mind as worry, fear, and anger. You might be afraid that the feelings will take over and never go away. This book can help you express yourself, and move on to a happier place.

Can you write what you think these six children are experiencing on the lines by their pictures? Are they feeling more than one thing? Ask your parent or friend if they think the same thing.

How it helps

Your body sends feedback to your brain about how things are going. By learning to recognize and interpret the feedback, you can tap into your system. Who is driving your super-powered machine? You are!

The Big Body Test

Does your whole body feel the same?
Or do different emotions affect different parts of you?
Make like a doctor and do a body scan to check yourself out.

Are you ready to have a conversation with your body, both inside and out?

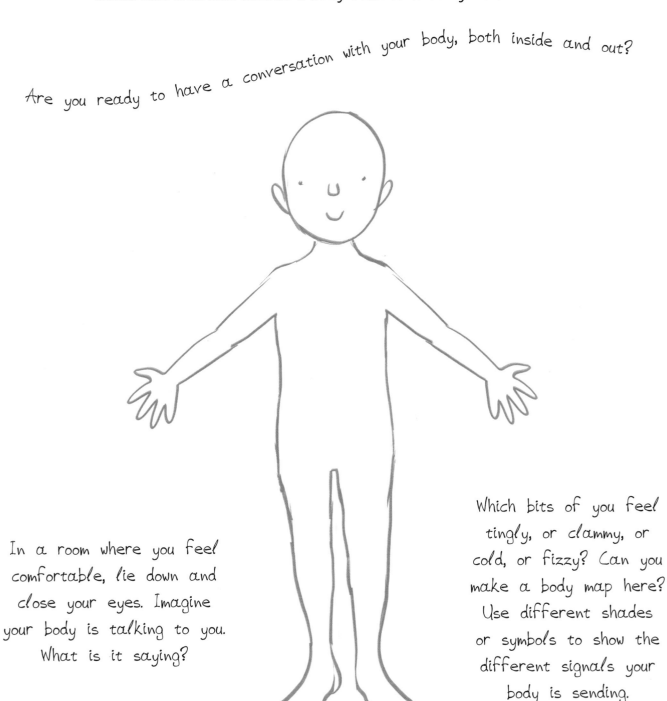

In a room where you feel comfortable, lie down and close your eyes. Imagine your body is talking to you. What is it saying?

Which bits of you feel tingly, or clammy, or cold, or fizzy? Can you make a body map here? Use different shades or symbols to show the different signals your body is sending.

For example, this boy is angry. It feels to him like an explosion in his head. This girl looks happy, but she is nervous. She knows this because it feels like she has butterflies fluttering in her belly.

How it helps

Sometimes our bodies know more than we do. Your heart, lungs, muscles, and skin are good at telling you how they feel. These things all work without needing you to tell them to, but you can also boss them around if you choose to.

Get a Move On

Your heart beats slowly when you're still, and speeds up with exercise. Put it to the test and see how it responds.

First, sit still. Put your first two fingers at the side of your neck, under your jaw. Can you feel the blip-blip-blip of your pulse? That is your heart telling you how hard it is working.

When you can feel a steady pulse, set a timer for 10 seconds. Count how many pulses you can feel. If you multiply that number by 6, you know how many times your heart beats in one minute.

Now stand up and do 25 jumping jacks, and then measure your heart rate again. It should be a higher number, because your heart is working harder.

Keep your fingers on your pulse and feel it slow down as you rest again. See how you're in control of the way your body behaves? What other activities do you do that make your heart beat faster? How long does it take to slow right back down to your resting rate?

How it helps

Your heart rate is one of the first signals of anger, threat, or upset. By getting good at feeling your heart rate you will know how keyed up or relaxed your body and mind are. And you can work to bring it down. Learning to observe your heart rate can bring you a sense of strength and control.

Heart rate at rest:
_____

How I moved:
_____
_____

Heart rate after exercise:
_____

Under Your Nose

What else can you use to make yourself happy? The answer is right under your nose ... it's your breath!

Begin by noticing your breathing. Sit quietly and close your eyes. Do you breathe in through your nose or mouth? How do you breathe out? Do you stop mid-breath, or breathe evenly and smoothly? Do you sometimes forget to breathe in or out?

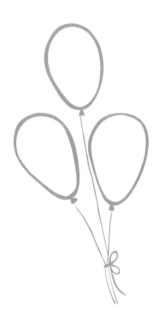

Breathing is an important part of your super-powered human machine. Learning to control your breath is one of the best ways to help you find your happy.

Now let's take control of your breathing. Put your hands on your belly and close your eyes. Imagine your belly is a balloon. Now breathe in slowly through your nose to fill your belly balloon. Push out your belly until it is big and full. Now breathe out through your mouth and let your balloon go small again. Repeat this four times. Do you feel different now?

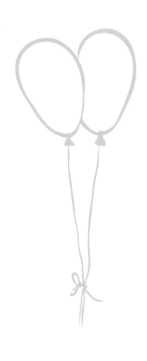

How it helps

Strong feelings can trigger physical reactions from head to toe. But you are not helpless. Breathing is the easiest and most effective way of managing your feelings. Regulating your breathing will regulate your heartbeat, your muscle tension, and strength, help you focus, and give you a sense of peace.

Make Lemonade

Now it's time to work your muscles. This movement is simple and fun to do, no matter where you are.

Sit or stand, and let your arms dangle loosely at your sides. Now squeeze your fists as tightly as you can. Imagine you are holding a lemon in each hand and squeezing the juice to make lemonade. Count to ten, and then let go. Repeat if you need to.

Focus on the difference between how your muscles feel when they are tensed and how they feel when they are relaxed. You can control how your muscles feel!

You can try this with other muscles in your body, too. Tense your belly and release it; make sure you don't hold your breath.

Try squeezing your bottom muscles together. These muscles are the biggest in your body, so you're doing some serious squeezing here!

How it helps

Your muscles hold your feelings without you knowing it. Sometimes they get stuck in a tense state. By intentionally contracting your muscles really hard, and then releasing them, you are burning the tension out of them and re-setting them to relaxed and happy.

Scan Your Skin

Your skin gives away your emotions, from sweating and blushing to goosebumps and chills. You can see your own skin, and touch it...but can you FEEL it?

Move your mind's eye over the skin on your whole body and see how it feels. Do you have sweaty palms or damp arm pits? Are your feet cold or clammy inside your socks? Is the back of your neck chilly, or prickly? Imagine that you are in a warm, dry desert. Let the hot sun make you toasty and warm, and dry any moisture that you don't want on your skin.

Treat yourself to some skin sensations. Put on your warmest socks or your softest clothes. Do you have a fleecy hoodie that's fluffy on the inside? If you're cold, take a warm shower and let the soothing water fall on your shoulders, or spend time in a lovely bubble bath. Snuggle into a soft towel and then curl up under a blanket.

How it helps

Tuning in to a specific part of your body (your skin, or your heart, muscles, or lungs, as on the previous pages) can help you really focus on the way your feelings affect you physically.

Weather the Storm

Your mood will change from day to day, from morning to evening, perhaps even from one hour to the next. It's even more changeable than the weather!

Rainy

Stop and think about how you feel right now. It can be hard to find the words. Instead, describe yourself like the weather. Are you feeling stormy, or sunny, or frosty, or gusty? What weather do you think each of these people are feeling like?

Snowy

Gloomy

Mia is feeling _____

Bright

Stormy

Maria is feeling _____

Drizzly

Marco is feeling _____

Cloudy

Sunny

Tyler is feeling _____

Windy

Noah is feeling ————————

Ania is feeling ————————

Draw your feelings on this chart. How do they change over a few days?

	Morning	Afternoon	Evening
Monday			
Tuesday			
Wednesday			
Thursday			
Friday			
Saturday			
Sunday			

Wait for the Calm

It's perfectly fine to feel down sometimes. People can't be happy all the time. When you have sad or angry feelings, it's important to notice them, and know that they will pass.

Write something that makes you feel sad or angry in each of these clouds.

How it helps

Writing down the triggers of our feelings gives our mind space to see things more clearly. By noticing and naming your feelings you give yourself distance to view them. You put your brain in charge and your feelings can stop running your life. When you write your feeling down, your feeling has done its job of telling your brain to act. Your brain says, "Understood, buddy. I'm on it." Try it.

Write something that makes you feel happy on each of the rainbows.

Don't try to ignore difficult feelings, as they're likely to hang around for longer.

What might make you feel better? Sometimes, a simple hug can help.

Be a Rainbow

Thinking about your breathing can brighten your day. Sometimes it is easier to focus on your breath if you imagine something real. Rainbows are beautiful and will help you to think happy thoughts.

1 Stand straight and still. Let your arms dangle at your sides, with your palms facing forward.

2 Lift your arms out to the side and then over your head, making a rainbow arch. Breathe in through the movement. Finish with your palms facing each other.

3 Reverse the action, making another rainbow as you lower your arms and turn your palms forward again. Breathe out and keep your actions floaty and light.

Close your eyes as you make the rainbow, and imagine each stripe—red, orange, yellow, green, blue, indigo, violet. Say them out loud if you like.

Draw some rainbows, too! We love rainbows!

How it helps

Linking your breathing with your movements helps your mind and body work together. Think about how you feel at the start, and whether you feel different after making rainbows.

Nature's Treasures

Are you feeling twitchy from being indoors for too long?
Is your mind too full of thoughts and questions?
Give your brain something to think about; go outside
and explore nature with a treasure hunt.

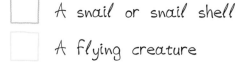

See how many of these things you can
find while you are out and about.
Tick them as you find them.

- ☐ A leaf with holes
- ☐ Purple petals
- ☐ A really smooth stone
- ☐ Lichen on a tree
- ☐ A fallen feather
- ☐ A spider's web
- ☐ Animal tracks
- ☐ An old log
- ☐ A snail or snail shell
- ☐ A flying creature

Find a space to sit and
listen. What sounds can you
hear? Are the birds singing?
Are the leaves swishing? Are
people nearby, talking or
animals rustling through the
undergrowth? Close your eyes if
it helps you to listen.

Being in nature is sometimes called "forest bathing."
Can you think why?

Can you find any nice-smelling flowers?

How it helps

Being in nature reduces negative feelings like stress, fear, or sadness. It increases the good feelings and makes us feel balanced. Scientists have found that just looking at trees can improve our mood.

Sail Away

You don't need to be near water to enjoy the feeling of rocking in a boat.
You can be a boat yourself to relieve tension and bring a smile to your face.

1 Lie flat on the floor on your belly.

2 Reach behind you and grab hold of your feet. Press your feet into your hands and gently pull your thighs and chest off the floor.

3 Rock forward and backward, like a boat on the ocean. You might find yourself holding your breath; release it and concentrate on breathing steadily the whole time.

How it helps

Notice how strong and bendy your body feels. Lying and rocking like this opens up your chest and lungs to help you breathe beautifully. It boosts your energy levels and helps you to fight off anxious feelings.

Think about where you would go to if you could sail anywhere in the world.
How happy would you be to explore new places?
Imagine yourself sailing home again, and landing safely back to shore.

Smiling Faces

Eating the right foods can lift your mood. Unfortunately, feeling down can make you choose the wrong foods. Make a conscious decision to eat well and feel better. Why not put a smile on your plate, too?

Buy some pizza dough, or make your own from a recipe or package. Follow the instructions (and enjoy the kneading stage!), and then roll it nice and thin and round. Spread tomato topping across it, then decorate it however you like. Try a smiley face, or a pretty pattern.

Draw your design here and copy it in the kitchen.

An assortment of bright fruits and vegetables gives you the best diet. Which foods can you think of for each box?

Red foods

Orange foods

Plan a pizza night with your whole family. What pizza designs will each person come up with?

Yellow foods

Purple foods

Green foods

How it helps

Feel-good foods can trigger chemicals in your brain that lift your mood. Carbohydrate-rich foods such as bread and pasta release serotonin, a natural chemical that cheers you up, but the feeling doesn't last very long. You need to regularly eat lots of fruits and vegetables to keep that happy feeling for longer.

Cooking, as well as eating, can make you feel good about yourself.

Secret Symbols

You might sometimes feel sad or worried in a crowd of people, and wonder what you can do to help that won't make everyone stare at you. Don't worry! There are some small things you can do without being noticed.

1 Make the shape of an O by touching your thumb tip with the tip of your pointing finger.

2 Now swap so your next finger touches your thumb tip.

3 Swap again to touch your third fingertip, and then your fourth.

4 Keep repeating the movement.

Peace—Calm—Safe—Happy

As you change fingers,
say these words in your head:
"Peace—Calm—Safe—Happy,"
or choose words
that you like.

How it helps

When you focus your thoughts on your fingers, and the words that go with
each finger touch, you replace those thoughts that are worrying you or making
you sad. Repeating something over and over again helps your body to accept it
and make it real.

Action Stations!

Staying still for too long can affect your mood. Hours and hours of gaming, watching TV, or reading a book might seem like fun, but it could drag you down. It's time to get up and get moving!

Set up a circuit with a variety of things to move and stretch your body. Have a go at each one five times. How do you feel?

Mountain climbers

Kneel down with your hands on the floor and your arms straight. Lift your bottom in the air and bend one knee to pull it in to your chest. Now straighten that leg and pull in your other knee. Repeat, as if you are running on all fours.

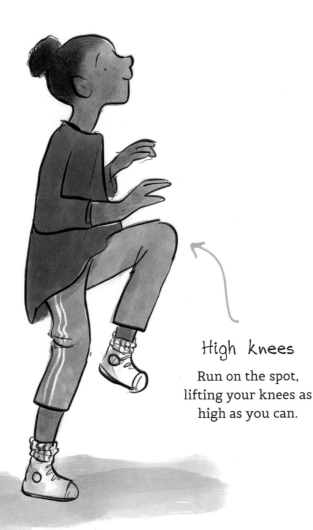

High knees

Run on the spot, lifting your knees as high as you can.

If your body isn't easily able to do any of these exercises, ask an adult to help you adapt the actions to better suit your body.

Can you persuade anyone else to join in? Encourage each other to keep going.

Bicycle kicks

Lie on your back on the floor. Touch your fingers to your ears. Slowly bring your left elbow near your right knee, straighten out again, and then bring your right elbow to your left knee. Keep moving like this and it will feel a bit like riding a bike.

Squats

Stand straight with your feet slightly apart. Look at the wall or window in front of you. Now, bend your knees and slowly drop your hips toward the floor, as if you are sitting down. Keep your bottom poked out. Push down on your heels as you stand up again.

How it helps

Moving around and raising your heart rate is exactly what your body needs every day. Our bodies aren't made to stay still for too long! Exercising actually changes your brain, helping it work better and feel better.

This Is Me!

How was your day? Did you feel a mixture of emotions and do a variety of things? What were the best bits? Were there any tough bits?

← Fill in this comic strip from start to finish.

This is me! Wakey-wakey!!

← Use the small boxes to show your mood. Was it sunny? Does it deserve a smiley face?

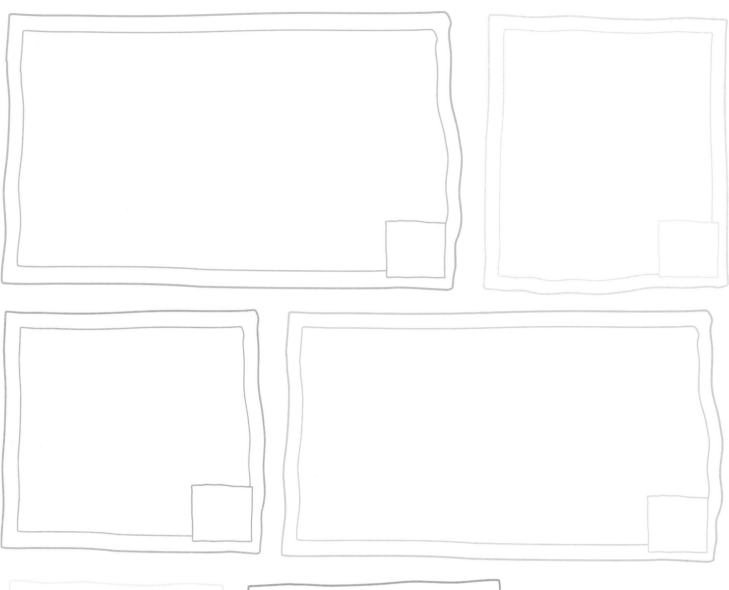

This is me!
Night night!

How it helps

It's important to take stock at the end of the day to see what parts went well and what parts were a struggle. You might start to see a pattern emerge! What part do you want to be better tomorrow?

Out and About

Being cooped up indoors all day can make you feel icky.
After a long day at school or at home, get back to nature
and have some fun in the fresh air.

Take a walk past trees or bushes. Are there any fallen leaves on the ground?

Pick a few up and use them to make patterns and pictures.

Don't forget to wash your hands before
you touch anything else.

If it's too wet or cold to go outside, draw nature patterns on the page instead. Try to sit by a window while you doodle.

How it helps

There's a reason we describe spending time outdoors as "getting some fresh air." The air really is fresher than the stale air inside a building. It cleans your lungs, frees up your body to work efficiently, and increases the amount of oxygen you inhale, which boosts your serotonin levels.

Be a Superhero!

Do you have superpowers? Hmm. Not many people do.
But you do have the power to change how your body feels
inside. You don't even need a cape or a magic hammer!

Lie down on your front. Raise your head and chest off the floor.

Lift your feet up slightly, and then point one arm in front as if you
are flying like a superhero.

What will you call your superhero alter-ego? You can even make a mask from paper and elastic, and a cape from an old towel!

Lie on your back and move your arms and legs as if you are crawling up a wall and across the ceiling.

Lie on your back again with your legs straight and arms by your sides. Let them lie loosely on the floor. Now squeeze all of your muscles tightly. Count to five and then focus your superpowers on relaxing all of your muscles. Keep repeating this until you feel more in control.

Shake It Off

Sometimes your mood dips a little bit, and you just need to refocus and have some silly fun. Taylor Swift was right about shaking it off—it's that simple!

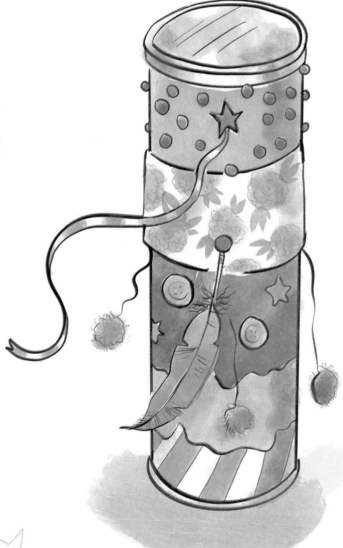

1 You will need a clean, empty food or drink container with a tight-fitting lid.

2 Carefully pour in a little bit of dry, uncooked rice. You don't need much—no more than 1/6 of the way up your container.

3 Replace the lid and seal it tightly with strong tape. Decorate the outside with more tape, giftwrap, paper, foil, ribbons, or anything fun you have lying around.

4 Now, shake, shake, shake. You can jump around and dance if you like, too!

Focus on your breathing while you dance and shake.

Try to make the rhythm of your breath match the rhythm of your shaking.

Breathe in through your nose and out through your mouth.

Don't hold your breath, as that will store up your worry chemicals again.

How it helps

Performing music, even simple rhythms like these ones, can lift your spirits. It has a physical effect on your body, reducing anxiety by releasing a chemical called dopamine, which controls the areas in your brain linked to pleasures and rewards.

Bear Hugs

When you're feeling blue, a big hug might help.
It isn't always easy to find someone and ask for
a cuddle, but that's okay. Learn to love yourself
with a big bear hug of your own.

Sit or stand with your
shoulders back and your arms
wide. Raise your chin a bit
and breathe in. Wrap your
arms around your body in
a big hug. Breathe out and
lower your chin. Hug—DONE!
But you can do it again and
again if you like!

The last time I needed
a hug I was feeling

After a hug I feel ...

Lie on your back and hug your knees to your chest. Squeeze them tightly and rock back and forth, from your head to your bottom. It's a hug and a back massage rolled into one!

How it helps

Your body responds to being held tight, and to physical touch, even if it comes from you. Taking time for a me-hug reminds you to look after yourself and be kind. Don't be too hard on yourself, and remember that other people value you as well.

People I like to hug

....

....

....

Scrunching your body into a small shape and then stretching it back out is a great way to release tension from your body. Notice how happy you feel when you open up.

Gifts from Nature

Sad feelings can drag your body down. Your head hangs low and you look at the ground. But there's always a silver lining. If you're feeling like that, keep your eyes open for precious treasures at your feet.

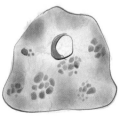 Next time you're out playing or walking, look for interesting stones and pebbles. Choose the ones you like the best and really enjoy them. Don't take them home—they belong where you found them.

Can you find a stone with a hole in?

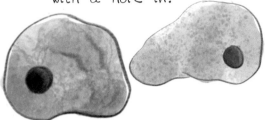

Search for the shiniest pebble.

Look for a stone with a stripe across it.

Find a smooth pebble that sits nicely in the palm of your hand (be sure to ask your parents or guardians where it's ok to take it from). Not too big, not too small. Just right!

1 Take it home and decorate it.
2 Use craft pens to add decorations to it, like bumps, swirls, or flowers.
3 Keep the pebble in your pocket and take it out when you're feeling downhearted, or keep it hidden but turn it around in your fingers or stroke it.

Try to find a white stone, a black stone, and all the shades in between.

How it helps

Playing with an item can distract you from your worries, and calm you to be able to cope with them. It can be comforting just to know your special stone is there.

Animal Instincts

Are you feeling like a bear with a sore head, as the saying goes? Or a hungry lion, an angry elephant, or a terrifying tiger? It's okay to be in a bad mood, especially if you're bored, or frustrated, or cross about something. Channel your inner animal to help you deal with the feelings.

Draw a picture of the animal you feel the most like right now:

Think about how your animal moves, and copy the action yourself. You could stomp like an elephant, or prowl like a tiger. Cover the whole floor with your crawling, creeping, crashing, or crouching.

How it helps

Your mood can be affected by things that you can't control. You can change your mood without changing the thing that caused it. You can be in control of your happiness, and getting outside your own head (and into an animal head, for fun) can help to make you happy.

Your Amazing Mind

Is your body uncomfortable, or is it your mind that's cranky? Can you tell the difference? Take your mind for a walk and leave your body behind! It takes practice, but you can do it.

Find a place where you can be still and quiet. Imagine yourself in a place that you love. Is it the beach, or a riverbank? Do you want to climb high and look down from the top of a mountain? You can go anywhere you like, so if you feel like swimming in the ocean among the whales, do it!

Imagine you aren't walking alone, but with someone you love. Do you hold hands, or run and skip together? Imagining good times can help when you feel low. Picture your most treasured people smiling or holding you tight.

How it helps

Your mind is a powerful tool. The image of your loved ones being nearby, without any judgement, can really lift your spirits. Imagine those people are walking with you, away from your yucky feelings and toward happy times.

Brighten Your Day

If you're feeling blue, what you wear can change your mood.
Picking your brightest top or wearing your best purple pants
can lift your spirits.

 Green is the shade of nature, and feels calming and healing. Wear it if you are feeling nervous about a new adventure.

 Light blue can be relaxing and can help if you struggle to sleep. Try blue PJs, or rest your head on a pale blue pillow.

 Yellow brightens up your thoughts. Wear it if your body or your brain is tired.

 Pink makes you happy! It brings out a smile from deep inside, and will make others smile as well.

 Orange is full of bounce and life. Use it to raise your energy levels when your body needs re-booting!

 Purple comes in different shades. The paler it is, the more soothing it is. Darker purple is intense and moody and can help if you're feeling flat.

 Red is a full-on, high-energy pick-me-up if you don't even want to get out of bed in the morning. Wakey wakey!

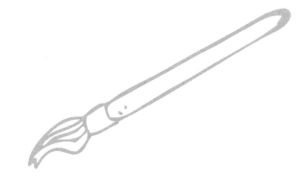

Which of the paint squares are you most drawn to today? Close your eyes and imagine the shade you have chosen. Picture it in front of you as you breathe in through your nose. Count to ten, breathing out through your mouth while imagining that you are blowing a bright ribbon away from you.

How it helps

Some shades are calming, while others are vibrant and uplifting. Your choice can influence your mood, or it can be a disguise to hide behind. If you wear yellow, people will treat you as if you are in a bright and sunny mood, even if you don't start out feeling that way.

Go Boom!

Sometimes feeling bored, or frustrated, or angry is okay, but you don't want the feeling to last too long. Let's turn your "meh" into merry with a mega-erupting volcano!

1 Tape a paper cup to a plate.

2 Cover the whole thing with kitchen foil and cut a cross in the top so you can fold the sides into the cup.

3 Place your shiny "volcano" on a large tray.

4 Pour 2 tablespoons of warm water into the cup, and then add a few drops of food dye, and 2 tablespoons of baking soda. Now slowly add up to 4 tablespoons of white vinegar, and watch the whole thing erupt!

How it helps

Trying out a new activity will take your mind off how you are feeling and give you something fun to focus on instead. And what better than an explosion? It shows you what can happen when feelings build up deep inside. It is often better to let them out instead of trapping them deep down. You wouldn't put a lid on a volcano, so you don't need to bottle up your emotions either. When you let yourself feel sad, or angry, you can deal with that emotion and then move on.

What has made your feelings go boom recently? Write it on this volcano,
and then use red and orange pens to make a mega eruption on the page.
Scribble until you feel lighter inside!

Making Faces

If you're bored, or irritable, or your sibling is getting on your nerves, then making some faces can help to clear out the twitchy feelings.

First, you're going to be a rabbit. Rabbits are cute, cuddly, bouncy, and definitely NOT fierce, angry animals. Sit up nice and straight on the floor or on a chair.

Twitch your nose like a bunny, and waggle your hands on your head for bunny ears. Scrunch up your face and then relax it.

Now imagine that you are a hungry rabbit, sniffing around for some food. Take three quick sniffs through your nose, then stop, and let out a big sigh through your mouth.

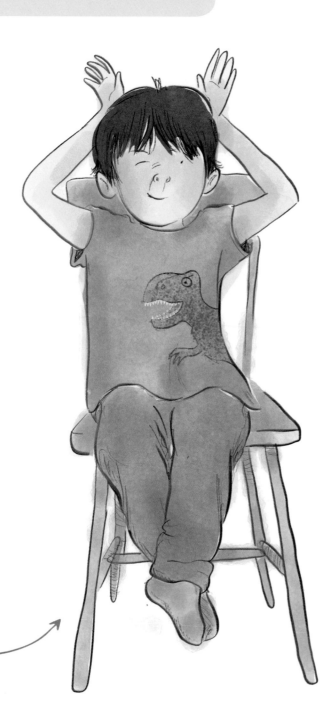

If you want to move around some more, try being a cat. Get on all fours and arch your back like a playful kitten. Take a deep breath in and then breathe out as you drop your back down again. Make meowing noises and open your mouth wide.

How it helps

Learning to stop, sit, and focus on your body is a great skill to have. You don't have to be all serious and frowny-faced about it—have fun with your face and your body. Concentrate on your breathing. A good breathing pattern will help you feel in control in all sorts of situations.

Just how loud can you meow?

See It, Say It!

Rather than focusing on the things that are making you sad, it might help if you think about the happier things you'd like to feel instead.

You're going to talk to yourself, so find a quiet space where you won't feel embarrassed. Sit or stand comfortably, preferably in front of a mirror. How do you want to feel? Choose one of the phrases here, or make up your own.

Today will be a good day.

I am clever and kind.

I believe in me.

How it helps

Positive statements make you feel positive. They can boost your belief in the good things and help you aim for the best. Saying the words over and over trains your brain to believe in that message.

What Makes Me Happy?

Do you know? Sometimes, looking for answers can make you see how many things there are to be happy about. Keep a record of your happy times to look at on a gloomy day.

Which of these would make you happy?

- ☐ Grandma took me to the park today.
- ☐ I emptied the dishwasher before I was asked to.
- ☐ I have fresh, clean sheets on my bed.
- ☐ I did well in my test at school.
- ☐ I tidied up after breakfast.
- ☐ My sister shared her cookies with me.
- ☐ I gave my old comics to my friend.
- ☐ We painted our nails.
- ☐ I found a stone with a cool hole in it.
- ☐ I chose my own clothes.
- ☐ Me and my brother/sister/friend played nicely while the grownups cooked.
- ☐ I licked the bowl after we made a cake.
- ☐ It snowed today!
- ☐ I tidied my toys away.
- ☐ Grandad bought me a muffin.
- ☐ I saw a fox running down the street.
- ☐ We went to the seaside.
- ☐ My friend has a new puppy.
- ☐ I learned how to climb a tree.
- ☐ We told silly jokes and couldn't stop laughing.
- ☐ We had hot chocolate with marshmallows.
- ☐ I've been invited to a sleepover.
- ☐ We had my best-ever meal tonight.

Write your own happy notes and keep them somewhere safe. You could keep them in a "happy jar." Next time you're sad, open the jar and remember some of the things that have made you happy before.

How it helps

Look at what you can do! Taking stock of your achievements can make you feel amazing. Aren't you kind? Aren't you lovely? Doesn't it feel great?!

Ooey Gooey Slime

There's nothing better to boost your mood than getting stuck in to some serious stirring … especially when the end product is slime. Pull it, squish it, stretch it, snap it; it's fantastic fun. You will need two special ingredients for this project, so plan ahead and stock up for days when only goo will do.

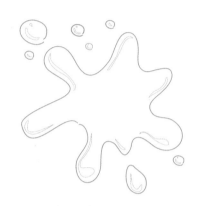

YOU WILL NEED:

- 1 small (115ml/4 oz) bottle of white PVA school glue
- 2 teaspoons baking soda
- a few drops food dye in any shade you like
- up to 5 teaspoons contact lens solution

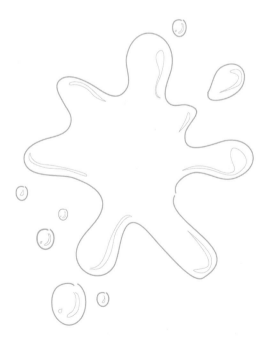

1 Pour the glue into a bowl and mix in the baking soda thoroughly.

2 Add food dye now and mix until you get the shade you like.

3 Add 3 teaspoons of contact lens solution and mix until it starts to get harder and slime begins to form.

4 Take the slime out of the bowl, and knead with both hands. If it's too sticky, add a few more drops of the contact lens solution.

Be sure to wash your hands
after playing with your slime!

Keep it in a sealed bag in the fridge.

Once your goo is formed,
you can experiment with it.
How does it feel? Is it cold?
How far will it stretch?
Can you cut it with scissors?
Can you draw on it?

How it helps

Playing with a touchy-feely substance like this uses the creative parts of your brain. That allows the bits of your brain that handle stress to take time off. The more you focus on your hands, the less you worry about any niggly thoughts that were churning round in your mind.

HALT!

How are you feeling? A bit sad, or a bit restless, or a bit droopy? What is causing you to feel like this? Try the HALT test to find out, and see what can make you feel better.

Close your eyes, take a deep breath, and ask yourself the four HALT questions:

Am I Hungry?
Am I Angry?
Am I Lonely?
Am I Tired?

If your answer is yes, then choose not to act negatively, but look for a way to feel better first.

Am I Angry?

Let out your anger like a lion. Get down on all fours and roar your head off. If there's anyone with you, warn them first: "Grandma, I need to do a lion roar. Don't be scared!"

Am I Hungry?

Easy peasy. Eat something that's good for you, such as an apple and cheese.

Am I Lonely?

Have a hug! Hugs always help. Find someone who loves you, or hug yourself. Go on—SQUEEZE!

Am I Tired?

Boost your energy levels with a short nap or some twitchy rabbit breaths (see page 56).

If you're feeling unsettled, lie down for a few minutes and imagine you are floating up, up, up on a puffy white cloud. Let it carry you away from any yucky feelings and then drift back down to Earth where you no longer feel tired, but happy.

How it helps

It's surprisingly easy to mistake everyday feelings such as hunger or tiredness for a much worse feeling. Emotions like loneliness and anger are temporary, and you can learn how to behave in a way that will send them packing and allow you to feel balanced again. It helps if you know how to identify the feelings in the first place.

Good Clean Fun

Do you feel like doing something naughty? How about drawing on the walls? Don't worry, parents, it won't make a mess!

You will need a can of shaving cream; it can be bought really cheaply, but ask before you use it. Now all you need is a smooth but unvarnished surface. A tiled wall, a window, a mirror, or a laminate table or worktop. That's it—there are no more rules. Squirt the foam and do your thing!

You can cover an area and draw pictures in it.

You can spray graffiti.

You can write your name.

Wipe over your designs and start all over again!

If your parents really aren't keen on you doing this, ask them to let you try next time you're in the bath or shower. It's guaranteed mess-free and safe!

How it helps

Letting loose feels great! Enjoy the feel of the foam under your hands and squishing through your fingers. Remember to clean up afterward. Doing the right thing also feels good!

Have a go here with some pencil doodles and scribbles.

Having a Laugh

If you're feeling down in the dumps, laughing is probably the last thing on your mind. However, if you force a smile and get giggling, it releases happy chemicals into your blood. Give it a go!

Look at yourself in a mirror and give yourself a grin. Now pull a silly face. Go on—really screw up your mouth and eyes and twist your nose. Stick out your tongue and try to touch your nose with it. Ask your dad to tell you his best (or most terrible) joke. Make yourself laugh even if it isn't that funny.

Enjoy the feeling—laughing is like giving all of your inside organs a big hug!

Write some of your most giggle-worthy jokes here!

DAD'S "BEST" JOKE

HA HA HA

SILLIEST JOKE

FUNNIEST JOKE

How it helps

Laughing makes your body relax and produce natural painkilling chemicals. However, your body can't tell the difference between real-life giggles and fake ones. Knowing how to force a laugh can help when you feel sad or stressed.

High Five

Over-thinking can make you worry or feel sad. If you find that the same thoughts are churning around and around, shift your attention to this activity instead.

Hold your hand in front of your face, at arm's length, palm facing out. Use the index (pointing) finger of your other hand to stroke up the outside length of your thumb. Breathe in to the top of your thumb, and breathe out as you trace down the other side. Keep breathing in and out as you go up and down each of your fingers. After five breaths, reverse it so you end up back at your thumb.

You could even draw a face on each finger. What are your characters called? Make up a personality for each of them, using your own best characteristics.

Breathe out

Breathe in

How it helps

Focusing on counting, breathing, and moving your finger gives your overactive mind something new, calm, and different to think about. It can be easier than just closing your eyes and trying to think of something else.

Use this technique to count to ten. Now how do you feel?

Learn From Other People

It is really easy to get caught up in your own emotions, and they can be overwhelming. Remember that everyone sometimes feels down— what can you learn from how other people deal with their feelings?

Ask a few friends or family members to keep a note of how they feel throughout a day (as Mia and Dad have done, here), then plot their feelings on the blank chart opposite. Use a different shade of pen for each person.

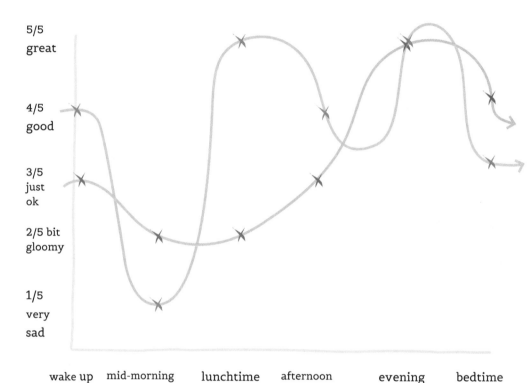

	5/5 great
	4/5 good
	3/5 just ok
	2/5 bit gloomy
	1/5 very sad

wake up　mid-morning　lunchtime　afternoon　evening　bedtime

Dad

7am	4/5	slept well, and got a run in before breakfast!
10am	1/5	car broke, late for work
1pm	5/5	met a friend for a walk at lunchtime, had a good chat
3pm	4/5	finished a project at work
5pm	5/5	pizza for dinner!!!
7pm	3/5	housework—not exciting, not awful

Mia

7am	3/5	slept ok, but was a bit late for school!
10am	2/5	didn't do too well in spelling test
1pm	2/5	didn't get to play the instrument I wanted in music class
3pm	3/5	paired with my friend for some group work in science class
5pm	5/5	pizza for dinner!!!
7pm	4/5	finished a hard book

Name _____

7am _____

10am _____

1pm _____

3pm _____

5pm _____

7pm _____

EVERYONE'S emotions are changeable, and that's okay.

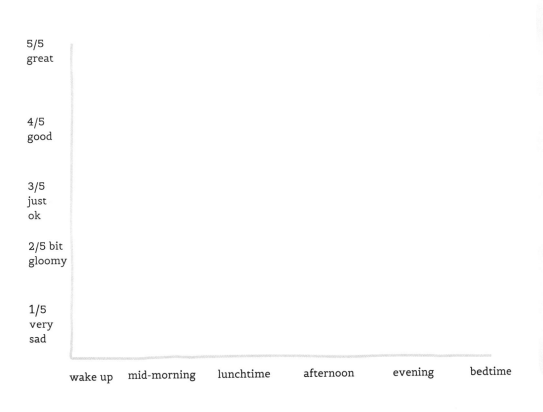

5/5
great

4/5
good

3/5
just
ok

2/5 bit
gloomy

1/5
very
sad

wake up   mid-morning   lunchtime   afternoon   evening   bedtime

How it helps

We all have lots of feelings every day, and they change all the time. It is important to recognize all of them, even the ones that make you unhappy, and to remember that you're not the only person who sometimes feels sad. Remember that a mood can pass, and remind yourself that you can change the way you feel because you're strong, and brave, and powerful.

Simon Says

Does your sad black cloud sometimes steal away your energy?
Bah! How dare it?! The best way to fight it is to move around.
Simon says so!

The rules to Simon says are simple. One person gives commands, and everyone else must follow—but only if the command begins with "Simon says." You can play with two or twenty-two people, as long as you have space to move around.

Add an animal twist to your game. Now Simon wants you to copy his furry, feathery, or fishy friends. Don't forget—you only carry out the action if Simon says. Concentrate!

Simon says:

Crawl like a caterpillar!

Scuttle like a crab!

Curl up like a mouse!

Stand on one leg like a flamingo!

Pounce like a cat!

Hop like a kangaroo!

Swoop like a vulture!

Slither like a snake!

Waddle like a penguin!

Clap like a sea lion!

Trot like a horse!

How it helps

Moving makes you feel good! It releases chemicals that cheer you up, help you unwind, and allow you to sleep better. Concentrating on the instructions will focus your mind as well as exercising your muscles.

Just Dance

Blow away your dark clouds with a blast of your top tunes. Music has the power to lift your spirits instantly, whether you're singing, listening, or dancing.

Turn on the radio or a music channel. What do you hear? Start to move ... sway to a slow tune or spin round to a fast song. Wave your arms and wiggle your bottom.

Indoors or outdoors, to music or to a tune inside your head, on your own or with your little sister—just dance!

Make a playlist of your happy tunes. Whenever you hear a song you like, write it down here, or add it to a "Happy Times" playlist in a music app. Listen to these tunes when you wake up, or travel to school, or once you're home; whenever you're feeling down or grumpy. Don't forget to do a little dance, if the mood takes you!

Pharrell Williams HAPPY

How it helps

Making a noise is an outlet for your emotions, both positive and negative. That's why anger can make people scream and shout, and people clap their hands when they're happy. Movement does the same job—we jump for joy, or throw things in a fit of rage. Use song and dance to channel any negative energy that's jiggling through your body.

Make a Rainbow Plate

Your body needs to be healthy physically so you can live your best life and do everything with energy and bounce. It is important to eat a wide variety of foods, and making a rainbow will help you get the right balance.

Fresh fruits and vegetables are important in so many ways. Some people don't eat anywhere near as many as they should. It can seem like an expensive way to eat, but these vital foods are no more expensive than sugary snacks or fast food.

1 Decide whether you are making a sweet rainbow with fruits, or whether you're in the mood for vegetables right now.

2 Think of foods that will make each stripe of your rainbow. Berries are great for filling each line, or try salad foods such as tomatoes, carrots, sweet peppers, celery, beets, and red cabbage.

3 Chop your foods into bite-sized pieces and arrange them on a plate. Delicious!

A rainbow of foods not only looks good, it tastes great and does you good, too. Share the love with your friends and family as one rainbow goes a long way!

How many different types of berries do you know? Have you tried them all?

Deep greens, vibrant reds, glorious yellows … they are all an indication that a food has different nutritional values. Eating a wide variety of fresh foods ensures that you get a good mixture of essential vitamins and minerals. Some of these, such as vitamins B and D, have been linked to mood-boosting chemicals made by your body.

How it helps

Sugary treats can make your mood swing from low to high and back again, and leave you feeling tired or grumpy. Healthy snacks can keep your body and mind in a stable, steady state. Taking time to prepare your food and have fun with it will help you enjoy eating it so much more.

A Big Thank You

How amazing are you? Pretty brilliant, if you stop and think about it. Often, though, we don't stop and think about it. We trudge along, and don't take notice of how astonishingly awesome our bodies really are. It's time to say thank you.

Sit or lie somewhere in a comfortable position. Imagine you are in a taxi and can get a ride to any part of your body. Where will you go? What is it like when you get there?

How wiggly are your fingers?
Are your toes warm or cold?
Is your face relaxed or tight?
Are your knees bent or straight?
Do you have any itches?
Is your belly rumbly or full?

As you travel around your body, think about what each part of you can do. Say thank you to it for helping you every day. Thank your arms for being strong, and your fingers for being nimble. If you love to run, say thanks to your legs for carrying you. If you love to do gymnastics, thank your body for being bendy but strong. Write a letter to your best body bits, and say thank you for the activities that you couldn't do without them.

How it helps

Every part of you plays a special part in getting you through the day, no matter how big or small. Sometimes it's good to stop and think and say thanks.

Take Tiny Steps

When you're feeling low, it can be hard to feel motivated to do anything. It's important to try, though. Even the smallest action is the start of something bigger.

Tiredness and lack of energy and motivation are some of the worst aspects of feeling down. However, just a small amount of activity will give your body enough of a boost to do more. It's an upward spiral that will make you feel better with every step along the way. Take a look through the activities in this book and choose one that sounds appealing. Ask a friend or family member to do it with you, if that helps.

Once you have taken the first step, look for a different type of task. If you worked your body with some stretches, now try something that benefits your mind, such as making up a story. Next, do something that is good for your heart and soul: reach out to another person and do something together. It will benefit both of you, and will break down those walls that your brain has been constructing that make you feel isolated and sad.

How it helps

You are a complex machine that has lots of different parts. You need all of them to work in harmony for you to be at your best. If one bit blips out, it upsets your whole self. That's why it works to try lots of different tasks that focus on your body, your mind, your heart, and your soul.

Find the Sunshine

Things can look very bleak and gloomy when your spirits are low. Here are some things you can try to break out of a pattern of negative thinking.

Look for something that went right, instead of dwelling on something you think went wrong.

Try not to see things as all or nothing, black or white, good or bad. There is always a middle ground of things that are just fine.

Remember: Every day, good things happen, to you and your loved ones, and the world around you.

How it helps

There is <u>always</u> something to feel positive about, and focusing on that can change your perspective, and leave you in a better frame of mind to deal with any problems.

Write down at least one good thing, no matter how small, that happened today.

Write down an idea of something easy you can do tomorrow to change things up a bit.

Break the cycle by doing something out of the ordinary.

It doesn't have to be a big thing—you could offer to take next door's dog for a walk, raise your hand in class, or wash up your plate after dinner.

If a friend of yours was feeling like you are now, what would you say to him or her? Write it down here. You're more likely to be able to look on the bright side to help another person.

For Parents

Why isn't your child happy?

Part of our job as parents is to give our children the tools they need to have good emotional health. People (including children!) who are emotionally healthy are in control of their thoughts, feelings, and actions. They are able to cope with life's challenges. They can keep problems in perspective and bounce back from setbacks. They feel good about themselves and have good relationships.

Being emotionally healthy does not mean a person is happy all the time. It means you are aware of your emotions, and you can deal with them, whether they are positive or negative. Emotionally healthy children (and adults!) still feel stress, anger, and sadness. But they know how to manage their negative feelings. They can tell when a problem is more than they can handle on their own. They also know when to seek help from other people.

Research shows that emotional health is a skill that can be learned. There are steps you can take to improve your child's emotional health and help him or her to be happier.

How can I tell if my child needs help?

You know your child better than anyone. How do you know if they are feeling seriously down? Do they tell you with words, or can you see it in their face and body language? The blues looks different in children than in adults. Here are some common ways kids express intense sadness:

- highly irritable
- refusing to talk
- indecisive
- tearful
- trouble concentrating
- overly sensitive to criticism
- not hungry or only wanting to eat sugary or high-fat foods
- grumpy and irritable
- sleeping more than usual
- uninterested in friends and family
- tired even after adequate sleep.

One of the best things we can do for our sensitive, sad child is to help them develop the ability to express their feelings. Research shows that being able to verbalize misery to a trusted loved one provides some relief right away. Simply stating our sad feelings out loud makes them not feel so awful. Listen and encourage your child with compassion and gentleness. Be patient. A sad child needs to process their feelings over time; and, their timeframe may not be the same as ours!

When to get professional help

When sadness goes on too long and starts to affect your child's functioning at home and school, it's time to seek outside help.

As a toothache signals time to go to the dentist, intensely sad feelings that last every day for more than two weeks should be treated by a doctor. It is best to intervene quickly so that depression does not take hold.

If you are worried about your child, your first step should be to visit your family doctor or arrange a consultation with your child's school. They will be able to give you some contact details tailored to the individual needs for your child, and your local facilities.

For Parents

Is it sadness or depression?

Sadness is a natural response to things like loss, illness, emotional strain, and disappointment. It allows the person to briefly disengage from the external world and focus inwardly to take stock and make a plan for changed circumstances. The bright side of sadness is that it helps the child take a break, build his or her energy back up, and make realistic plans and goals.

Fight

Depression can look a lot like sadness from the outside. It's a condition that raises the levels of stress hormones, which causes physical changes. It's all down to the body's "fight, flight, or freeze" responses to real or imagined danger.

Freeze

When a person feels under threat, their body prepares to run, or stand and face the danger. Their heart begins to beat faster to pump blood into their muscles. It deprives the brain of oxygen, making the sufferer feel restless and unable to concentrate.

With depression, some chemical systems in the brain stop working properly, including the serotonin system. Serotonin has been nicknamed the happy chemical, as it contributes to well-being. It also regulates the appetite and sleep patterns.

Flight

What's going on?

Scientists are still unsure what's going on inside the brain during depression. Scans show that the parts of the brain involved in sleep, appetite, and mood all look different for a depressed person. It can be brought on by external factors, such as stress, illness, and grief. However, it can appear from nowhere, and may be linked to changes in hormone levels or certain genetic characteristics.

For Parents

How you can help

Learning emotional regulation is a life-long journey, and you play a vital role in your child's development.

1 Do a basic needs check

Is your child hungry, tired, sick, frustrated, or bored? Sometimes a simple snack, an early bedtime, changing an activity, or tucking her under a cozy blanket and taking her temperature may be all that is needed.

2 Lend a listening ear

Sometimes sad feelings take on a life of their own and the child can no longer identify what caused their sadness. Help them make a list of the times when they felt happy. Focus on those for a few minutes. Let them know that you are there to listen if they want to talk. When your child does talk to you, be sure that you are receptive to how they are feeling. Don't brush it aside or tell them not to worry. Instead, let your child know that it's okay to feel rough, but that you can look for solutions together. Ask open-ended questions that make them really think about what their worries are.

3 Be a supportive presence

Sometimes just sitting together in the same room is enough to lift a sad child's mood. And don't forget to hold them or gently read to them or sing if they would like that. A good hug can go a really long way to feeling better.

4 Encourage movement

As long as your child isn't sick, remember that we are made for movement. Moving our muscles literally lifts our spirits by stimulating the release of feel good hormones like serotonin. What the movement is doesn't matter, so if your child feels like riding a bike, going for a swim, or digging a hole in the backyard for a fairy pond, support them in doing it. The positive feelings generated by exercise can drive out negative ones.

5 Remember, it takes a village to raise a child!

Your child may benefit from talking to someone else they trust. Point them in the direction of a teacher, a relative, or a helpline with trained counsellors. Exposure to a wide variety of viewpoints will give your child the best chance of responding to a point of view that clicks with them. They might (or might not) talk to an aunt or friend of yours. Let your child help out a relative with a task, and see if they start chatting.

6 Limit exposure to negative stimuli

Research shows that watching TV shows with arguing, fighting, shooting, car accidents, ridicule, death, and loss affect the viewer's brain as if they experienced these things directly. Have your child generate his or her own entertainment through making puppet shows, writing stories, or playing charades. When they do need "down time" play pleasant instrumental music, or have them do a puzzle, draw, or read. These activities bring a great sense of peace, and diminish preoccupation with sad storylines.

7 Good sleep and regular diet

Do your part by ensuring that your child is well fed and well rested. Good nutrition and a regular sleep pattern are vital for a growing child, particularly one who is struggling with sad feelings. A child aged 6–12 needs 10–11 hours sleep every night. Eat healthy food and occasional treats together as a family.

8 Help your child set a small goal

Lazing about breeds sour feelings when you are down. Achieving a goal does wonders for morale. Pick out an activity from this book and help your child get started. Simple beading and baking projects lead to a sense of accomplishment, as does tidying up a drawer.

How to use this book

Use this book to help find coping mechanisms, whether that is breathing exercises, calming skills, physical activities. or other targeted distractions. Unfortunately, today's children often need guiding into the pastimes that came more instinctively to previous generations—heading outdoors, losing yourself in nature, and letting off steam, or curling up quietly to read or draw. These, though, are the ventures that a child needs to be able to turn to when their mood and energy levels drop and their spirits are low.

For Parents

How you can help (continued)

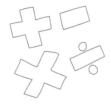

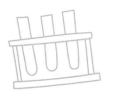

9 Let them be kids!

Don't overload their childhood days with clubs and lessons. Have faith in their schooling and the professionals who know how hard children should be working at their age. Allow your kids time to play and unwind, and encourage them to spend time with their peers and siblings. Try to allow them some totally unstructured time most days, and let them do anything they would like, provided that it is safe, doesn't inconvenience you, and is within your budget.

10 Drink plenty of water

Teach your child the importance of drinking water throughout the day. Dehydration can affect our mood as well as our brain function and physical performance.

11 Happy energy is contagious

Cheerful parents tend to create optimistic home environments. Parenting an unhappy child can be exasperating and stressful. There is no shame in struggling with feeling down yourself. Find another adult to talk to and engage in some self care. If you are able to keep your cool and lighten the mood by not taking everything too seriously, allow yourself to be silly and laugh. By watching you, your child will gain perspective on the intensity of their brooding feelings and may be able to laugh, too.

12 Set a routine

Routine is important in helping children to feel safe and grounded. A good morning routine will set the tone for the day. Get up early enough to avoid chaos and fluster; eat a good breakfast; go through what they need so they feel supported and prepared for the day ahead. Bedtime routines are equally comforting, and can include stretches and a bedtime story to settle them both physically and mentally.

And finally,

Remember to set a good example! Be aware of how you may seem to your child. Do you have a positive outlook and a cheerful approach to the things that life throws at you? Do you avoid moaning or wallowing in the negative? Let them know that you tackle obstacles and deal with problems on a daily basis, but that it can be done without letting things get you down. And remember those cuddles … they are beneficial to you as well as to them!

Glossary

balanced
To feel stable in both body and mind with few high and low feelings.

carbohydrate
Food that is made up of sugars and starches that are a main source of energy.

conscious
Being aware of something. To make a conscious decision is to know exactly what you are doing and why.

contracting
Pulling together to become shorter.

dopamine
A chemical in the brain that sends messages to other parts of the brain and body. It contributes to the feelings of wellbeing, pleasure, and reward.

feedback
A response that gives you useful information. For example, when you cut yourself, your body sends a message to your brain to send healing chemicals to the wound.

flexible
To be able to adapt to change with positivity.

heart rate
Another name for your pulse or the beats of your heart.

keyed up
Wound up or feeling tense and agitated.

lichen
A type of crusty flat plant that grows on tree trucks and stones.

minerals
Substances found in food (like vitamins) that are important for a healthy body and brain, such as calcium which gives you strong bones and teeth.

mood
A temporary state of mind or a general feeling, such as sadness or happiness.

motivation
The desire to do something for some kind of reward, which could be money, or to achieve a goal, to please someone, or just to feel good.

nutritional values
The amount of goodness that is in a certain food, such as the quantity of fat or protein.

outlet
A way out for your feelings and self-expression.

perspective
A viewpoint or way of seeing something.

playlist
A collection of songs or tunes that are put in a certain order to be played on the radio, a phone or another device.

pulse
The beats of your heart.

serotonin
A chemical in the body that sends messages to the brain and gives you a feeling of wellbeing and happiness.

threat
A danger or something you think might cause you harm.

triggers
Causes something to happen.

vibrant
Bright, full of life or energy.

vitamins
Substances found in food (like minerals) that are important for a healthy body and brain, such as vitamin C, which prevents colds and other illnesses.

Further Reading

You can also ask your family doctor for advice or consult a psychologist if you would like more information or mental health resources for kids.

My Family Divided: One Girl's Journey of Home, Loss, and Hope, Diane Guerrero with Erica Moroz

In My Heart: A Book of Feelings, Jo Witek, illustrated by Christine Roussey

My Many Colored Days, Dr. Seuss, illustrated by Steve Johnson and Lou Fancher

Tough Guys (Have Feelings Too), Keith Negley

When Sophie Gets Angry — Really, Really Angry…, Molly Bang

North America

kidshealth.org
With sections for parents, kids, and teens, this is what most pediatricians use for education.

www.girlshealth.gov
A website specifically for girls, this has lots of great information about feelings, relationships, and biology.

healthfinder.gov
Mostly for parents, this has lots of good advice articles.

adaa.org
The specific website of the Anxiety and Depression Association of America.

worrywisekids.org
Accessible to both kids and adults, this is a great source of information on anxiety and depression.

UK

Childline
Help and advice about a huge range of issues. Comforts, advises, and protects children 24 hours a day, and offers free, confidential conselling by helpline, online chat, and Ask Sam. Tel: 0800 1111 www. childline.org.uk

The Samaritans
Listening and support for anyone who needs it. Contact 24 hours a day, 365 days a year—calls and emails are free and confidential. Tel: 116 123 www.samaritans.org

NHS
www.healthforkids.co.uk/feelings/
You can always talk to your family GP about your feelings.

Australia & New Zealand

Kids Helpline (telephone and online counselling for ages 5–25)
kidshelpline.com.au/ or call 1800 55 1800

Youthline
www.youthline.co.nz
Free call 0800 376 633
Free text 234

Index